Linux in 3 Days

Day 1

Copyright © 2022
All rights reserved.

Contents

Introduction
Day 1
Getting Access
Getting Connected
Welcome to Shell
Linux Directory Structure
Basic Linux Commands
Teach Yourself to Fish
Working with Directories
Listing Files and Understanding ls Output
What's Next
About the Author
Other Books by the Author
Additional Resources Including Exclusive Discounts for You
Appendices
Appendix A:
Abbreviations and Acronyms

Appendix B: FAQ
Appendix C: Trademarks

INTRODUCTION

As the founder of the Linux Training Academy and an instructor of several courses, I've had the good fortune of helping thousands of people hone their Linux skills. Interacting with so many people who are just getting started with the Linux operating system has given me invaluable insight into the particular struggles and challenges people face at this stage.

One of the biggest challenges for people interested in learning the ins and outs of Linux is simply a lack of time. When you are working with a limited and extremely valuable resource you want to make sure you make the most of it.

The next biggest challenge for Linux newcomers is knowing where to start. There is so much information available that deciding what to focus your attention on first is a big enough hurdle to keep many people from even starting. What's worse is starting down the path of learning only to discover too many concepts, commands, and nuances that aren't explained. This kind of experience is frustrating and leaves you with more questions than answers.

That's why I've written this book.

Not only have I condensed the most important material into five sections, each designed to be consumed in a day, I've also structured the content in a logical and systematic manner. This way you'll be sure to make the most out of your time by learning the foundational aspects of Linux first and then building upon that foundation each day.

In *Learn Linux in 5 Days* you will learn the most important concepts and commands, and be guided step-by-step through several practical and real-world examples. As new concepts, commands, or jargon are encountered they are explained in plain language, making it easy to understand.

Let's get started.

DAY 1

GETTING ACCESS

In order to start learning your way around and putting your newfound knowledge to the test, you're going to need access to a Linux system. If you already have an account on a Linux system, you can skip ahead to the next chapter.

Web Hosting Shell Accounts

If you use a web hosting service to host your website you may already have a Linux account that you can use. Consult your hosting company's documentation and search for "SSH" or "shell access." SSH stands for Secure Shell and it provides a way to connect to a server over a network, like the Internet. If you don't already have a web hosting provider, you can sign up for one and use it for shell access. Shared web hosting providers typically charge just a few dollars a month.

Here are some shared web hosting companies that can provide you with a shell account and SSH access.

- [1and1.com](1and1.com)
- BlueHost.com
- DreamHost.com
- HostGator.com
- Site5.com

Using Preinstalled Linux Images

VirtualBox is virtualization software that can be installed on Windows, Mac, Solaris, or Linux. It allows you to run an operating system (guest) inside your current operating system (host). It's more time consuming than the other options, but it can be worth the extra effort to have your own personal Linux system. In this scenario you will spend a few minutes installing the virtualzation software, downloading a pre-installed Linux image, and importing that image.

To get started, head over to the VirtualBox download page located at https://www.virtualbox.org/wiki/Download

s and grab the installer for your current operating system. Click through the install screens and accept the defaults.

Next, download a virtual disk image (VDI) from http://virtualboxes.org to use. I recommend that you download a CentOS or Ubuntu image unless you already know which Linux distribution you will be working with in the future. Honestly, you can't make a wrong decision. The concepts that you will be learning in this book apply to any Linux distribution.

Launch VirtualBox, create a new virtual machine, and use the virtual disk image that you just downloaded. When you are asked for a hard disk image select the "Use existing hard disk" radio button and click on the directory icon. Next, click "Add" and select the virtual disk image. When the virtual machine is powered on you can log into the server using the username and password provided with the downloaded image.

Deep Dive

These links along with other supplemental material is available at:

http://www.linuxtrainingacademy.com/lfb

- How to Install VirtualBox on Mac - A video that guides you through the installation of VirtualBox on Mac.
  http://youtu.be/xBQdflx1L1o
- How to Install VirtualBox on Windows - A video that guides you through the installation of VirtualBox on Windows.
  http://youtu.be/CBhppdewtEQ
- VirtualBox Documentation - Official VirtualBox documentation
  https://www.virtualbox.org/wiki/Documentation
- VirtualBox download page - Where to obtain a copy of the VirtualBox software.
  https://www.virtualbox.org/wiki/Downloads
- VirtualBoxes.org - A good source of virtual disk images.

http://virtualboxes.org/

GETTING CONNECTED

When your account is created you will be provided with details on how to connect to the Linux server. You may be provided with some or all of the following information:

- Username. This is also known as an account, login, or ID.
- Password
- SSH key
- Server name or IP address
- Port number
- Connection protocol

The connection protocol will either be SSH (Secure Shell) or telnet. SSH and telnet provide ways to connect to a server over the Internet or a local area network. In the vast majority of cases the connection protocol will be SSH. Telnet is practically obsolete at this point, however you may run into it if you need to access a legacy system.

Choosing an SSH Client

If you were given a specific SSH client to use, use that program and follow the documentation for that product. If you are free to choose your own client or were not provided one, I suggest using PuTTY for Windows or Terminal for Mac.

PuTTY can be downloaded from this website: http://www.LinuxTrainingAcademy.com/putty/. You only need putty.exe to get started.

The Terminal application comes pre-installed on Macs and is located in the /Applications/Utilities folder.

A list of other SSH clients is provided in the Deep Dive section at the end of this chapter.

Connecting via SSH with a Password from Windows

To connect to the Linux server using the SSH connection protocol, launch PuTTY.

Type the host name or IP address you were given into the Host Name (or IP address) box. If no port was given to you, leave it at the default value of 22.

Enter your username by clicking on Data in the left pane. It is located directly below Connection. Type your username into the Auto-login username field. If you skip this step you will be prompted for your username when you connect to the server.

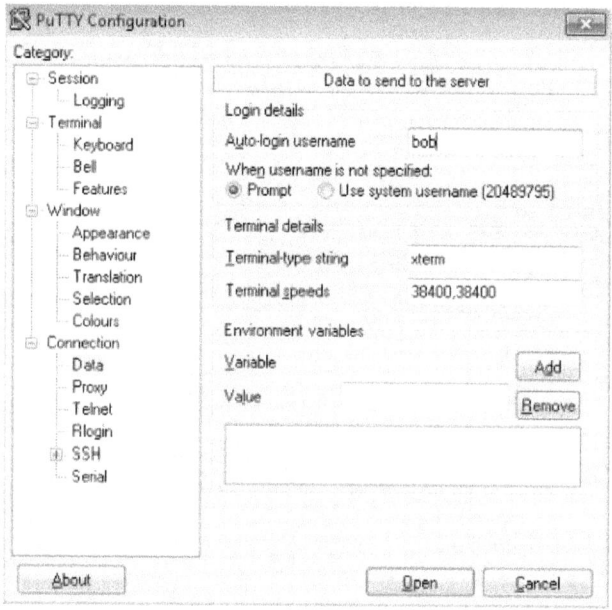

Save your session by typing in a name in the Saved Sessions box and clicking Save. This allows you to speed up this process by simply double clicking on your saved session to connect to the Linux server.

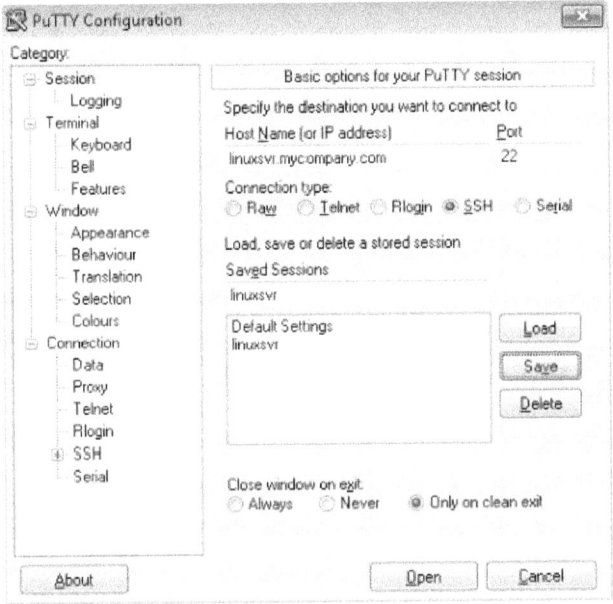

When you click Open a connection attempt will be made. The first time you connect to a particular server, PuTTY will ask to cache that server's host key. You will not be prompted again on subsequent connections. To add the server's SSH host key to PuTTY's cache, simply click Yes when prompted.

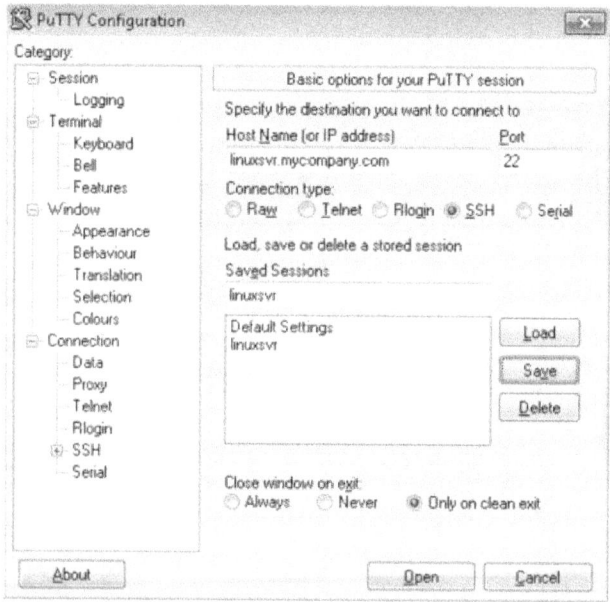

Once you are successfully logged in, you will see something similar to this:

Connecting via SSH with a Password from Mac

The built-in SSH client on Mac is a command line program. Command line programs can be run with the Terminal application that comes with the Mac operating system. It is located in the /Applications/Utilities folder. The format of the ssh command is ssh -p port_number username@servername . If you were not provided a port number, then the default port of 22 is assumed and you can omit -p 22 from the ssh command. Similarly, the username only needs to be specified if it is different on the server than it is on your Mac workstation. For example, if your username on your Mac is bob and your username on linuxsvr is also bob, you can omit bob@ and simply type ssh linuxsvr. Once Terminal is running, type in the ssh command. Commands are case-sensitive and the ssh command is lowercase. It should look like one of these three options:

ssh linuxsvr
ssh bob@linuxsvr
ssh -p 2222 bob@linuxsvr

The first time you connect to a particular server you will be asked to verify that server's host key. You will not be prompted again on subsequent connections. When you are asked Are you sure you want to continue connecting (yes/no)? type yes and press Enter. Once you have established a connection, you will be prompted for your password.

```
air:~ bob$ ssh bob@linuxsvr
The authenticity of host 'linuxsvr (10.0.0.7)' can't be established.
RSA key fingerprint is cc:d8:f0:cf:c2:34:1a:69:80:7e:ad:c2:23:df:b9:4f.
Are you sure you want to continue connecting (yes/no)? yes
Warning: Permanently added 'linuxsvr,10.0.0.7' (RSA) to the list of known hosts.
bob@linuxsvr's password:
[bob@linuxsvr ~]$
```

Like Mac, Linux also comes with a terminal program and an SSH client. Once you are connected to one Linux server you can use the ssh command to connect to another Linux server. You can nest multiple connections and navigate through your network of Linux servers in this fashion.

General Information on Connecting via SSH with Keys

You may have not be given a password, but rather given an SSH key or even asked to generate one. In the physical world a key unlocks a door. Similarly, an SSH key is used to unlock the access to your account on a server. If you do not have a key, you cannot unlock the door.

Using account passwords or a combination of account passwords and SSH keys is a common practice. With the growth of cloud computing in recent years, it is becoming more and more popular to use SSH keys exclusively. Since cloud servers are often connected to the public internet, they are prone to brute force attacks. A mischievous person could write a program that repeatedly connects to your server trying a new username and password combination each time. They can increase their odds of gaining entry by using a list of common usernames and passwords. Configuring your cloud server to not accept account passwords and to only accept SSH keys eliminates this threat.

You can further increase the security of your SSH key by giving it a passphrase. In this case it takes something you have -- the key -- and something you know -- the passphrase -- to gain access to your account. If you feel confident that your key will only be under your control, you can forgo providing a passphrase for your key. This will allow you to log into servers without typing a password at all. Having an SSH key without a passphrase can allow you to automate and schedule tasks that require logging in to remote systems.

Importing SSH Keys on Windows

If you were given an SSH key that is not already in the PuTTY format, you will need to convert it. PuTTYgen is required in order to convert an SSH key on a Windows system.

Run PuTTYgen, click Load and navigate to the private SSH key you were given. The names of the files are typically id_rsa or id_dsa for private keys, and id_rsa.pub or id_dsa.pub for public keys.

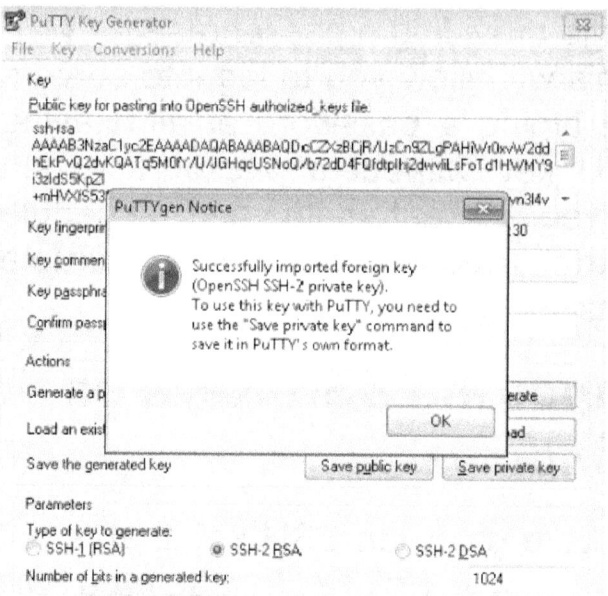

Now you can save the public and private keys for later use with PuTTY.

Generating SSH Keys on Windows

In order to create an SSH key on a Windows system, you will need PuTTYgen.

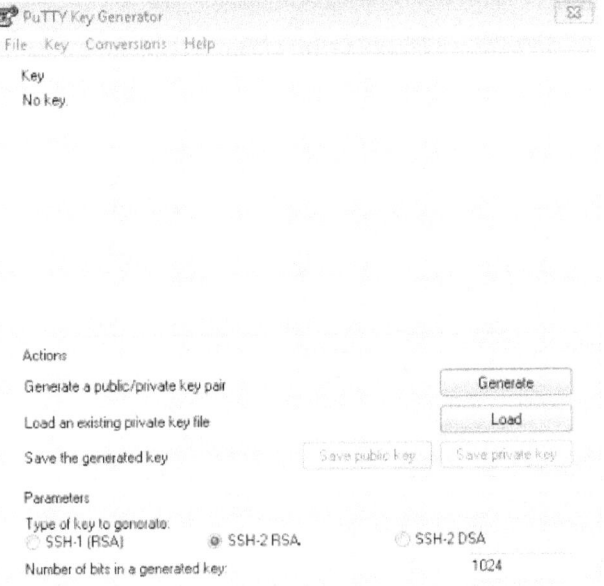

When you run PuTTYgen you will be asked to move the mouse around to create some random data that will be used in the generation of the key.

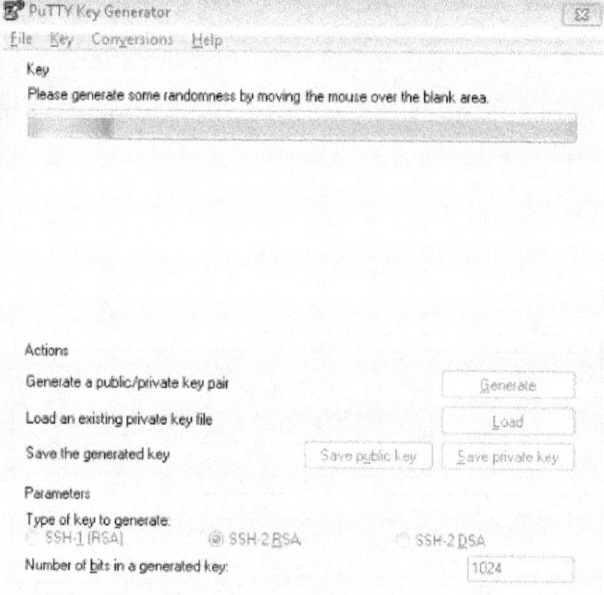

You have the option to use a passphrase for your key. You can also change the comment to something more meaningful like Bob's key .

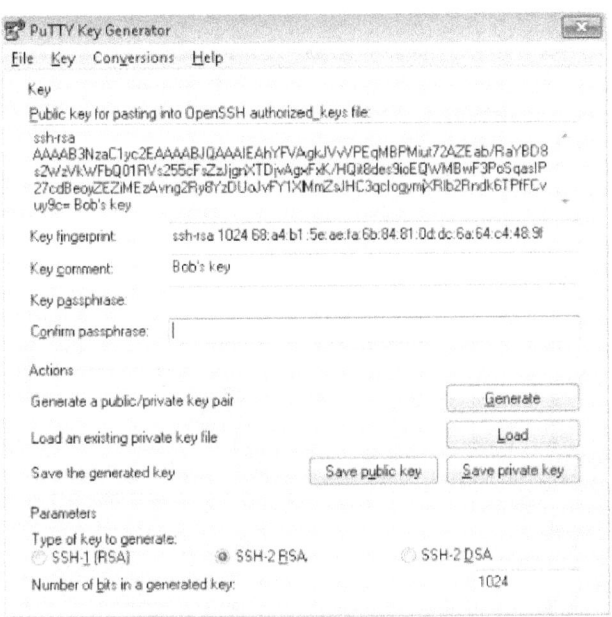

Now, save the public and private keys buy pressing Save public key and then Save private key . Give the public key to the system administrator so they can associate it with your account. The private key is for your eyes only. Do not share your private key!

Next, export the key as an OpenSSH key by clicking on Conversions and then Export OpenSSH Key. This OpenSSH key can later be used on Unix or Linux systems.

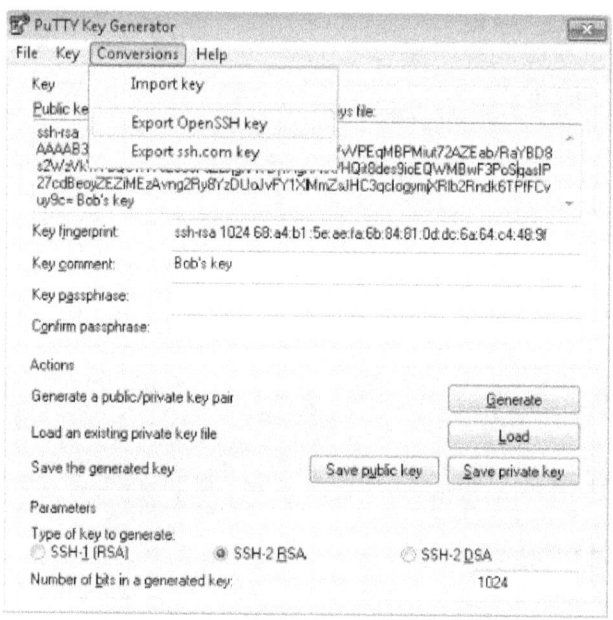

Connecting via SSH from Windows

Follow the "Connecting via SSH with a Password from Windows" instructions, but this time add one additional step to specify your SSH private key file. You can do this by by clicking on the plug sign (+) next to SSH in the left pane to reveal more options. Next click on Auth. In the right pane select Browse under the Private key file for authentication field and locate your private SSH key.

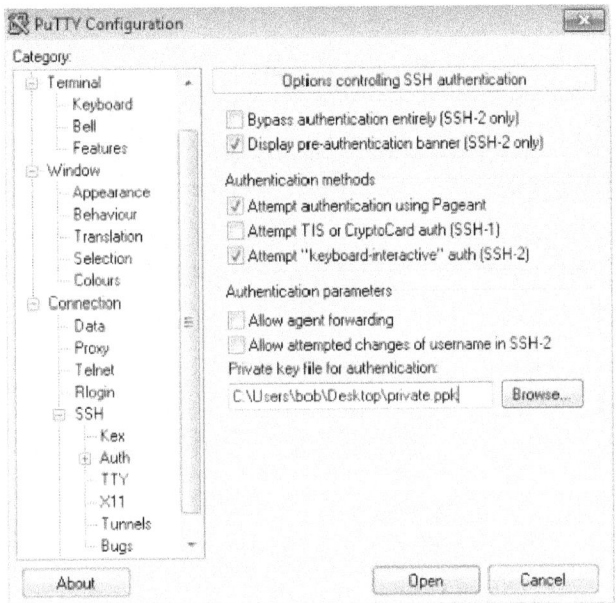

Generating SSH Keys on Mac

If you are asked to generate an SSH key, launch the Terminal application and use the command line utility named ssh-keygen. You will be asked a series of questions. Accept all the defaults by pressing Enter. Optionally enter a passphrase for your SSH key.

```
mac:~ bob$ ssh-keygen
Generating public/private rsa key pair.
Enter file in which to save the key
(/Users/bob/.ssh/id_rsa):
Enter passphrase (empty for no passphrase):
Enter same passphrase again:
Your identification has been saved in
/Users/bob/.ssh/id_rsa.
Your public key has been saved in
/Users/bob/.ssh/id_rsa.pub.
The key fingerprint is:
0b:14:c5:85:5f:55:77:35:5f:9e:15:a9:b4:b0:54:0
5 bob@mac
The key's randomart image is:
+--[ RSA 2048]----+
|      .o.o. .E+=@|
|      .o o.. oO|
|      . ...+ o.o|
|       .  .. o  |
|        . S     |
|         ..     |
|          .     |
|                |
|                |
+----------------+
```

Connecting via SSH with Keys from Mac

If you generated your keys, this part is already done for you. If you were given an SSH key, you need to place it in a directory named .ssh underneath your home directory. Open the Terminal application and type in the following commands. Press the Enter key at the end of each line.

mkdir ~/.ssh
chmod 700 ~/.ssh

You will gain a full understanding of what these commands do as you progress through this book. In order to expedite the process of getting connected, the details will be saved for later.

Switch to the Finder to copy your keys into the .ssh folder. In the Finder menu click Go and then Go to Folder... and type ~/.ssh when prompted. When you click go, the .ssh folder will be displayed. Now you can drag your keys into place.

```
Go to Folder

Go to the folder:
~/.ssh

                          Cancel    Go
```

Back in the Terminal window, set the proper permissions on your key files. (Again, these commands will be covered later.)

cd ~/.ssh
chmod 600 *

I highly recommend naming the keys in the following format: id_rsa and id_rsa.pub or id_dsa and id_dsa.pub Otherwise, you will have to specify the location of your key when you use the ssh command or perform some additional configuration to tell SSH that your keys are not named in the standard way.

As a general rule it makes your life much easier if you follow the standard conventions and common practices. I will point them out along the way. One of the things I love most about Linux is the freedom and power it gives you to do things in a myriad of ways. There are cases where not following the standard conventions will be the right thing to do.

If you still wish to name your key something else, you can tell SSH where to find it by adding -i key_location to the ssh command. Remember, the format of the ssh command we used above is ssh -p port_number username@servername. It can be expanded to ssh -i key_location -p port_number username@servername. Here's an example:

ssh -i /Users/bob/.ssh/bobs_key bob@linuxsvr

Connecting via Telnet

Telnet used to be the de facto way to connect to a Unix or Linux server. Over the years telnet has been replaced with Secure Shell, abbreviated SSH. SSH is, as its name implies, more secure than telnet. Telnet sends your login credentials over the network in plain text. SSH encrypts the communications between the client and the server, thus greatly improving security. If someone were to be packet snooping or eavesdropping on your connection, they would see garbled text and random characters. If you do have a need to telnet to a system you can use the SSH instructions from above, but with a couple of minor changes.

Connecting via Telnet from

Windows

Run PuTTY and select the Telnet radio button. If no port was given to you, leave it at the default value of 23. You will be prompted for your username and password when you connect to the server.

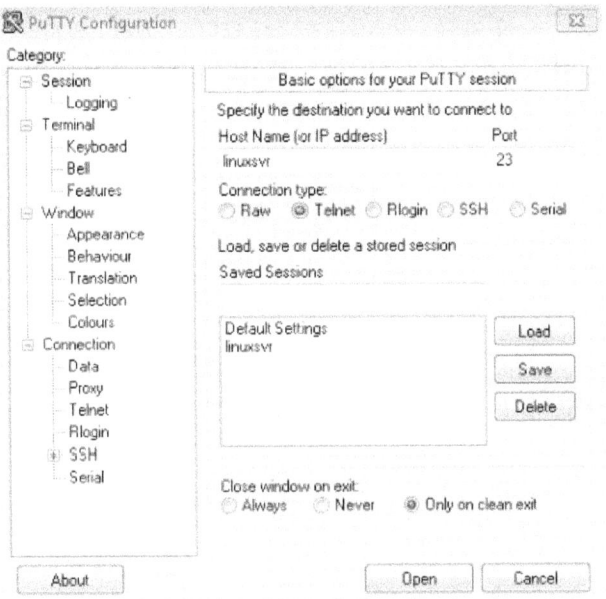

Connecting via Telnet from Mac

The built-in telnet client on Mac is a command line program. Command line programs can be run with the Terminal application that comes with the Mac operating system. It is located in the /Applications/Utilities folder. The format of the telnet command is telnet servername port_number . You only need to include a port number if it is different than the default value of 23. You will be prompted for your username and password when you connect to the server.

```
mac:~ bob$ telnet linuxsvr
Trying 10.0.0.7...
Connected to 10.0.0.7.
Escape character is '^]'.
Ubuntu 12.04.3 LTS
linuxsvr login: bob
Password:
Last login: Thu Nov  7 01:26:37 UTC 2013
Welcome to Ubuntu 12.04.3 LTS

* Documentation:  https://help.ubuntu.com/

System info as of Nov 7 01:26:52 UTC 2013

System load:  0.42
Usage of /:   3.1% of 40GB
Memory usage: 32%
Swap usage:   0%
Processes:         89
Users logged in:   0
IP address for eth0: 10.0.0.7

bob@linuxsvr:~$
```

Connecting Directly

If you are running Linux in VirtualBox as described in the previous chapter or you have dedicated hardware with Linux installed on it, you can simply log in directly to the server. You will be presented with a prompt requesting your username and password. If it is a graphical environment, you will need to find a terminal application to use after you have logged in. In most cases it will literally be "terminal", but you might see some slight variations like "gnome terminal", "konsole", or "xterm."

Here is what opening the terminal application looks like in CentOS. You will find it in one of the menus.

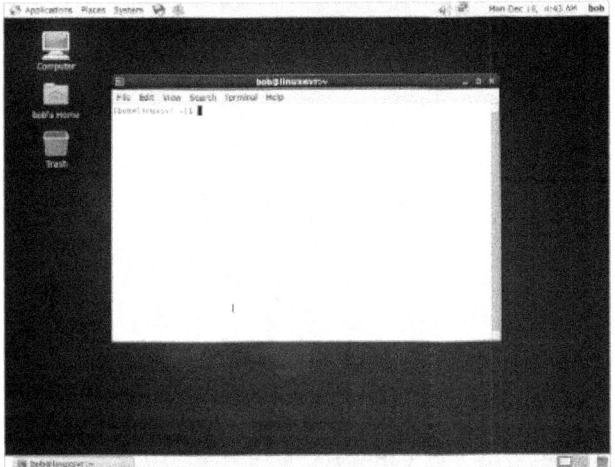

In some Linux graphical environments there may not be a traditional menuing system. In these cases you will want to search for the terminal application. In this Ubuntu example, click the button in the top left of the screen to bring up the dashboard. You can now start typing to find applications that are installed on the system.

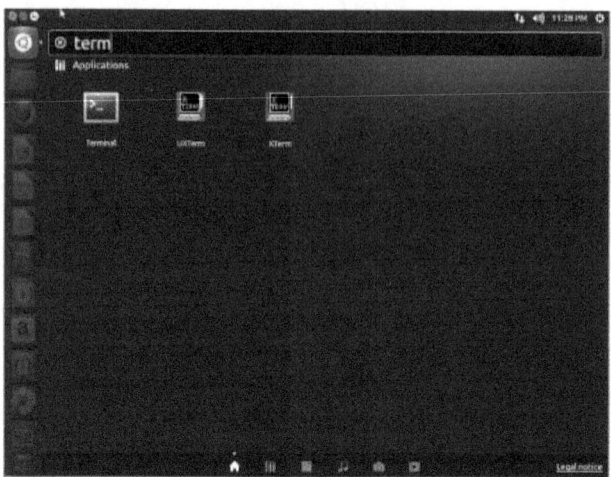
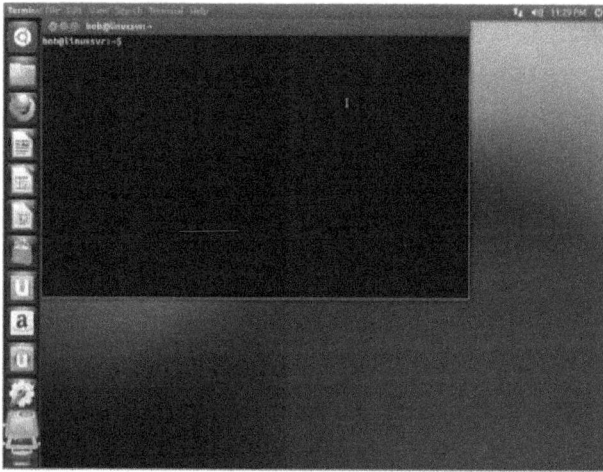

Deep Dive
- List of Mac SSH clients http://www.openssh.org/macos.html
- List of SSH clients, all platforms http://en.wikipedia.org/wiki/Comparison_of_SSH_clients
- List of Terminal Emulators - Includes terminals for Windows, Mac, and Linux. http://en.wikipedia.org/wiki/List_of_terminal_emulators
- List of Telnet Clients https://en.wikipedia.org/wiki/Telnet#Telnet_clients
- List of Windows SSH clients http://www.openssh.org/windows.html
- OpenSSH.org - The official website for OpenSSH.
- PuTTY http://www.LinuxTrainingAcademy.com/putty/
- Watch Star Wars over a telnet connection.

- telnet towel.blinkenlights.nl
- To disconnect, hold down the Ctrl key and press the right bracket ( ]). At the telnet > prompt type quit and press Enter .
* Using SSH Public Key Authentication http://macnugget.org/projects/publickeys

WELCOME TO SHELL

When you log into a server over the network the shell program is started and acts as your default interface to the system. The shell is nothing more than a program that accepts your commands and executes those commands. Said another way, the shell is a command line interpreter.

Let's look at the shell prompt you'll be working with. The prompt just sits and stares at you waiting for you do something interesting like give it a command to execute. Here is Bob's shell prompt.

bob@linuxsvr $

Bob's prompt is in a common format of username@servername $. In this example, the prompt is displaying the username, the server name, and if that user is using the system as a normal user ($) or a superuser (#).

The superuser on a Linux system is also called root. Anything that can be done on a server can be done by root. However, normal users can only do a subset of the things root can do. Root access is typically restricted to system administrators, but if you happen to support an application on a Linux server you may need root privileges to install, start, or stop it. There are ways to grant specific users root privileges for specific cases. This is often accomplished with the sudo -- SuperUser Do -- program. That will be covered later. For now, just know that most of your day to day activities will be performed using a normal user account.

Your prompt might not look like Bob's. Common items that appear in prompts include the username, server name, present working directory, and the current time. Here are a few more prompt examples.

[bob@linuxsvr /tmp]$
linuxsvr:/home/bob>
bob@linuxsvr:~>
[16:45:51 linuxsvr ~]$
$
%
>

In two of the prompt examples you will notice a tilde (~). The tilde is a shorthand way of representing your home directory. In this example the tilde (~) is equivalent to /home/bob , which is Bob's home directory. This is called tilde expansion. A username can be specified after the tilde and it will be expanded to the given user's home directory. For example, ~mail would expand to the home directory of the mail user which is /var/spool/mail . Another example is ~pat expanding to /home/pat .

Prompts do not have to be contained on a single line. They can span multiple lines as in the following examples.

linuxsvr:[/home/bob]
$

(bob@linuxsvr)-(06:22pm-:-11/18)-]-
(~)

[Mon 13/11/18 18:22 EST][pts/0][x86_64]
<bob@linuxsvr:~>
zsh 14 %

 linuxsvr   Mon Nov 18
06:22pm

~/

For the remainder of this book the prompt will be shortened to the dollar sign ($) unless displaying the full prompt provides additional clarity. Also, the default prompt may vary from system to system, but you can customize it to your liking. That, along with other shell related topics, is covered in a later chapter.

Deep Dive

- Tilde Expasion
  http://gnu.org/software/bash/manual/html_node/Tilde-Expansion.html

LINUX DIRECTORY STRUCTURE

Now that you are able to connect to the server and have been introduced to the interface you will be using, it's time to learn about the directory layout. Understanding the directory structure will help you in the future when you are searching for components on the system. It can help you answer questions like:

Where are programs located?

Where do configuration files live?

Where might I find the log files for this application?

Common Directories

Here are the most common top level directories that you need to be aware of and may interact with as a normal user.

| Dir | Description |

Dir	Description
/	The directory called "root." It is the starting point for the file system hierarchy. Note that this is not related to the root, or superuser, account.
/bin	Binaries and other executable programs.
/etc	System configuration files.
/home	Home directories.
/opt	Optional or third party software.
/tmp	Temporary space, typically cleared on reboot.
/usr	User related programs.
/var	Variable data, most notably log files.

Comprehensive Directory Listing

Here is a comprehensive list of top level directories that you may find on various Linux systems. Some subdirectories are included to help clearly define the purpose of the top level directory. You may never interact with many of these directories. Some of these directories will be on every system you encounter like /usr . Other directories are unique to specific Linux distributions. You can safely skim over this list and refer back to it if or when you have a practical need to do so.

Dir	Description
/	The directory called "root." It is the starting point for the file system hierarchy. Note that this is not related to the root, or superuser, account.
/bin	Binaries and other executable programs.
/boot	Files needed to boot the operating system.
/cdrom	Mount point for CD-ROMs.
/cgroup	Control Groups hierarchy.
/dev	Device files, typically controlled by the operating system and the system administrators.
/etc	System configuration files.

Dir	Description
/export	Shared file systems. Most commonly found on Solaris systems.
/home	Home directories.
/lib	System Libraries.
/lib64	System Libraries, 64 bit.
/lost+found	Used by the file system to store recovered files after a file system check has been performed.
/media	Used to mount removable media like CD-ROMs.
/mnt	Used to mount external file systems.
/opt	Optional or third party software.
/proc	Provides information about running processes.
/root	The home directory for the root account.
/sbin	System administration binaries.
/selinux	Used to display information about SELinux.

Dir	Description
/srv	Contains data which is served by the system.
/srv/www	Web server files.
/srv/ftp	FTP files.
/sys	Used to display and sometimes configure the devices and busses known to the Linux kernel.
/tmp	Temporary space, typically cleared on reboot. This directory can be used by the OS and users alike.
/usr	User related programs, libraries, and documentation. The sub-directories in /usr relate to those described above and below.
/usr/bin	Binaries and other executable programs.
/usr/lib	Libraries.
/usr/local	Locally installed software that is not part of the base operating system.
/usr/sbin	System administration binaries.

Dir	Description
/var	Variable data, most notably log files.
/var/log	Log files.

Unix Specific Directories

Linux is often found in environments with other Unix variants. If you ever have a need to log into a Unix server you may see some of the following Unix specific directories.

Dir	Description
/devices	Device files, typically controlled by the operating system and the system administrators.
/kernel	Kernel and kernel modules. (Solaris)
/platform	Platform specific files. (Solaris)
/rpool	ZFS root pool directory. (Solaris)
/net	Used to mount external file systems. (HP-UX)
/nfs4	Used to mount the Federated File System domain root. (Solaris)

Dir	Description
/stand	Files needed to boot HP-UX.

Note that you may encounter other top level directories that have not been listed above. However, those were most likely created by the system administrator.

Application Directory Structures

Applications can follow the same conventions employed by the operating system. Here is a sample directory structure of an application named apache installed in /usr/local .

Dir	Description
/usr/local/apache/bin	The application's binaries and other executable programs.
/usr/local/apache/etc	Configuration files for the application.
/usr/local/apache/lib	Application libraries.
/usr/local/apache/logs	Application log files.

Here is what it might look like if it was installed in /opt .

Dir	Description
/opt/apache/bin	The application's binaries and other executable programs.
/opt/apache/etc	Configuration files for the application.
/opt/apache/lib	Application libraries.
/opt/apache/logs	Application log files.

A common alternative to placing all the application subdirectories in /opt/app-name is to also use /etc/opt/app-name and /var/opt/app-name . Here is what that might look like for our example apache application.

Dir	Description
/etc/opt/apache	Configuration files for the application.
/opt/apache/bin	The application's binaries and other executable programs.
/opt/apache/lib	Application libraries.

Dir	Description
/var/opt/apache	Application log files.

Sometimes applications that are not part of the standard operating system are installed in a shared manner and are not given their own subdirectory. For example, if apache was installed directly into /usr/local its binaries would live in /usr/local/bin and its configuration would live in /usr/local/etc . Apache may not be the only locally installed software so it would share that space with the other installed applications.

Another common practice is to create a directory structure based on a company, organization, or team name. For example, if you work at the Acme Corporation you may find a directory named /opt/acme or /usr/local/acme .
Sometimes scripts and utilities are installed directly in that structure and other times there are segregated into their own subdirectories. Here's an example.

Dir	Description

Dir	Description
/opt/acme	Company top level directory.
/opt/acme/bin	Binary programs created by or installed by the Acme Corporation.

Alternatively you may see something like this.

Dir	Description
/opt/acme	Company top level directory.
/opt/acme/apache	The top level directory for Acme's installation of apache.
/opt/acme/apache/bin	The apache binary programs.

Here are variations on the same idea, but based on a team within the company.

Dir	Description
/opt/web-team	The web support team's top level directory.

Dir	Description
/opt/acme/web-team	The web support team's top level directory.
/usr/local/acme/web-team	The web support team's top level directory.

Example Top Level Directory Listings

Here is a listing of the top level directories for a few different Linux servers. Listing files and directories with the ls command will be covered in the next chapter.

Red Hat Enterprise Linux 7 (RHEL)

```
[bob@rhel6 ~]$ ls -1 /
bin
boot
cgroup
dev
etc
home
lib
lib64
lost+found
media
mnt
opt
proc
root
sbin
selinux
srv
sys
tmp
usr
var
```

SUSE Linux Enterprise Server 11 (SLES)

```
[bob@sles11 ~]$ ls -1 /
bin
boot
dev
etc
home
```

lib
lib64
lost+found
media
mnt
opt
proc
root
sbin
selinux
srv
sys
tmp
usr

Ubuntu 14.04 LTS

[bob@ubuntu12 ~]$ ls -1 /
bin
boot
dev
etc
home
lib
lib64
lost+found
media
mnt
opt
proc
root
run
sbin

selinux
srv
sys
tmp
usr
var

Deep Dive

- Filesystem Hierarchy Standard
  http://refspecs.linuxfoundation.org/FHS_2.3
- man hier
- RedHat Enterprise Linux
  http://redhat.com/products/enterprise-linux/
- SUSE Linux Enterprise Server
  https://www.suse.com/products/server/
- Ubuntu
  http://www.ubuntu.com/

BASIC LINUX COMMANDS

Here is a short list of basic, but essential commands. In Linux, commands are case-sensitive and more often than not they are entirely in lowercase. Items that are surrounded by brackets ([]) are optional. You will more than likely use at least some of these commands every time you log into a Linux system. Become familiar with these commands because they can get you pretty far in a short amount of time.

ls - Lists directory contents. You will use ls to display information about files and directories.

cd [dir] - Changes the current directory to dir . If you execute cd without specifying a directory, cd changes the current directory to your home directory. This is how you navigate around the system.

pwd - Displays the present working directory name. If you don't know what directory you are in, pwd will tell you.

cat [file] - Concatenates and displays files. This is the command you run to view the contents of a file.

echo [argument] - Displays arguments to the screen.

man command - Displays the online manual for command . Type q to quit viewing the manual page. The documentation provided by the man command is commonly called "man pages."

exit , logout , or Ctrl-d - Exits the shell or your current session.

clear - Clears the screen.

Here is a screen capture of Bob's session using the above commands.

```
$ ls
PerformanceReviews sales-lecture.mp3
sales.data tpsreports
$ cd tpsreports
$ pwd
/home/bob/tpsreports
$ ls -l
total 2
-rw-r--r-- 1 bob users 31 Sep 28 14:49 coversheet.doc
```

```
-rw-r--r-- 1 bob users 35 Sep 27 08:47 sales-report
$ cat sales-report
We sold lots of widgets this week!
$ echo $PATH
/bin:/usr/bin:/usr/sbin:/usr/local/bin
$ man ls
NAME
       ls - list directory contents
...
```

More details on how you can fully exploit the power of these simple commands will be covered later. But right now, grab your fishing pole -- you're about to learn how to fish.

TEACH YOURSELF TO FISH

Knowing where executable commands live and the man command can take you a long way. You can teach yourself how to use Linux with this method, but it would be a long, slow process. More often than not, the man command will be used as a quick reference. It would be nearly impossible to memorize every option for every command and there is no need to do so when you have the man command at your fingertips.

To get help for the man command type the letter h while viewing a manual page. That will give you a list of commands you can use to navigate or search. Here is the concise version.

Enter - Move down one line.

Space - Move down one page.

g - Move to the top of the page.

G - Move to the bottom of the page.

q - Quit.

An environment variable is a storage

location that has a name and a value. The one we are interested in at the moment is PATH . The PATH environment variable contains a list of directories that contain executable commands. You can determine the value of PATH by prepending it with a dollar sign ($PATH) and using the echo command to display its value to the screen.

$ echo $PATH
/bin:/usr/bin:/usr/sbin:/usr/local/bin

When you type in a command at the prompt and press Enter , that command will be searched for in the directories in your $PATH . In this example, /bin will be searched first. If the command is found it will be executed. If it is not found, then /usr/bin will be searched and so on. If no executable command is found that matches your request, you will be politely told that it cannot be found.

$ whatsupdoc
-bash: whatsupdoc: command not found

If you want to know exactly where a command is located you can use the which command. If the program cat is located in /usr/bin and in /usr/local/bin , the one which will get executed depends on your $PATH .

```
$ which cat
/bin/cat
$ which tac
/usr/bin/tac
```

Putting this all together, you can start looking at what is in each directory in your $PATH and use the man command to discover what each one of them does and how to use them. Remember, to exit the man command type the letter q .

```
$ echo $PATH
/bin:/usr/bin:/usr/sbin:/usr/local/bin
$ cd /bin
$ ls
awk diff cal cat cp date du echo grep groups less more
$ man diff
NAME
      diff - compare two files
...
$ cd /usr/bin
$ ls
clear crontab cut dos2unix find kill mv pstree pwd sed strings touch ...
$ man touch
```

Note that the output of the

above ls commands was truncated. In reality there can be hundreds of commands in /bin and /usr/bin .

Many commands will provide hints for how to use them at the command line. Some commands will accept the -h flag, others will accept --help , and some will refuse to give you any help at all.

$ cal -h

Usage:
cal [options] [[[day] month] year]

Options:
-1, --one   show only current month (default)
-3, --three   show previous, current and next month
-s, --sunday   Sunday as first day of week
-m, --monday   Monday as first day of week
-j, --julian   output Julian dates
-y, --year   show whole current year
-V, --version   display version information and exit
-h, --help   display this help text and exit
$ diff --help
Usage: diff [OPTION]... FILES
Compare files line by line.

  -i --ignore-case Ignore case differences in file contents.

--ignore-file-name-case Ignore case when comparing file names.
...

If you are not sure what command to use, you can search through the man pages with man -k KEYWORD . From there you can read the man page for the command or ask it for help with -h or --help .

$ man -k calendar
cal   (1) - display a calendar
zshcalsys (1) - zsh calendar system

Deep Dive

- ExplainShell - Type in a command-line to display help for each item.
  http://explainshell.com/

- Getting Help From Linux - An article from the Linux Journal on using man pages.
  http://www.linuxjournal.com/node/1022962

- LinuxManPages.com - This website allows you to search man pages or browse a category of commands and man pages.

http://www.linuxmanpages.com/

- Linux commands broken down by category.
  http://linux.math.tifr.res.in/manuals/categories-index.html

WORKING WITH DIRECTORIES

Directories are simply containers for files and other directories. They provide a tree like structure for organizing the system. Directories can be accessed by their name and they can also be accessed using a couple of shortcuts. Linux uses the symbols . and .. to represent directories. Think of . as "this directory" and .. and "the parent directory."

Symbol	Description
.	This directory.
..	The parent directory.
/	Directory separator. Directories end in a forward slash and this is often assumed.

The directory separator is optional for the last subdirectory in a path or command. For example, the following commands work identically.

$ cd /var/tmp
$ cd /var/tmp/

Using the shortcuts can make navigating

easier. For example, type cd .. to go to the directory just above your current directory.

```
$ pwd
/home/bob
$ cd tpsreports
$ pwd
/home/bob/tpsreports
$ cd ..
$ pwd
/home/bob
$ cd ..
$ pwd
/home
$ cd .
$ pwd
/home
```

The cd . command did not take you anywhere. Remember that . is "this directory" and .. is "the parent directory." Another shortcut for navigating directories is cd - . This command takes you to the previous directory. The environment variable that represents your previous working directory is OLDPWD . So, cd - and cd $OLDPWD are equivalent.

```
$ pwd
/home/bob
$ cd /var/tmp
```

```
$ pwd
/var/tmp
$ echo $OLDPWD
/home/bob
$ cd -
/home/bob
$
```

How would you execute a command that is in your current directory? Assume your current directory is your home directory. By default your home directory is not in your $PATH . Here is how to do that.

```
$ ./program
```

Why does that work? Well, . represents "this directory", / is the directory separator, and program is the program to execute. You can always use the full path to be explicit. Here are two ways to execute program .

```
$ pwd
/home/bob
$ ./program
$ /home/bob/program
```

Creating and Removing Directories

The mkdir command is used to create

directories and the rmdir command removes them.

mkdir [-p] directory - Create a directory. Use the -p (parents) option to create intermediate directories.

rmdir [-p] directory - Remove a directory. Use the -p (parents) option to remove all the specified directories. rmdir only removes empty directories. To remove directories and their contents, use rm.

rm -rf directory - Recursively removes the directory and all files and directories in that directory structure. *Use with caution.* There is no "trash" container to quickly restore your file from when using the command line. When you delete something, it is gone.

```
$ mkdir newdir
$ mkdir newdir/product/reviews
mkdir: Failed to make directory "newdir/product/reviews"; No such file or directory
$ mkdir -p newdir/product/reviews
$ rmdir newdir
rmdir: directory "newdir": Directory not empty
$ rm -rf newdir
$ ls newdir
ls: newdir: No such file or directory
$ pwd
/home/bob
$ cd ..
$ pwd
/home
```

LISTING FILES AND UNDERSTANDING LS OUTPUT

Here is the output from an ls command using the -l option. The -l flag tells ls to display output in a long format. If you need to see what files or directories exist, use ls. However, if you need detailed information use ls -l.

$ ls -l
-rw-rw-r-- 1 bob users 10400 Sep 27 08:52 sales.data

On the far left of the ls output is a series of characters that represent the file permissions. The number that follows the permissions represents the number of links to the file. The next bit of information is the owner of the file followed by the group name. Next the file size is displayed followed by the date and time when the file was last modified. Finally, the name of the file or directory is displayed. Here is the information displayed by the ls -l command in table form.

| Item | Value |
| Permissions | -rw-rw-r-- |

Item	Value
Number of links	1
Owner name	bob
Group name	users
Number of bytes in the file	10400
Last modification time	Sep 27 08:52
File name	sales.data

The meaning of -rw-rw-r-- will be covered in detailed in the "File and Directory Permissions Explained" chapter.

Listing All Files, Including Hidden Files

Files or directories that begin with a period (.) are considered hidden and are not displayed by default. To show these hidden files and directories, use the -a option.

$ ls -a

.
..
.profile
.bash_history
lecture.mp3
PerfReviews
sales.data

tpsreports

Up until this point when you have used options, you have preceded each option with a hyphen (-). Examples are -l and -a . Options that do not take arguments can be combined. Only one hyphen is required followed by the options. If you want to show a long ls listing with hidden files you could run ls -l -a or ls -la . You can even change the order of the flags, so ls -al works too. They are all equivalent.

$ ls -l
total 2525
-rw-r--r-- 1 bob sales 25628 Sep 27 08:54 lecture.mp3
drwxr-xr-x 3 bob users 512 Sep 28 09:20 PerfReviews
-rw-r--r-- 1 bob users 10400 Sep 27 08:52 sales.data
drwxr-xr-x 2 bob users 512 Sep 28 14:49 tpsreports
$ ls -l -a
total 2532
drwxr-xr-x 4 bob sales 512 Sep 28 14:56 .
drwxr-xr-x 14 root root 512 Sep 27 08:43 ..
-rw-r--r-- 1 bob users 28 Sep 28 14:22 .profile
-rw------- 1 bob users 3314 Sep 28 14:56

.bash_history
-rw-r--r-- 1 bob sales 25628 Sep 27 08:54 lecture.mp3
drwxr-xr-x 3 bob users 512 Sep 28 09:20 PerfReviews
-rw-r--r-- 1 bob users 10400 Sep 27 08:52 sales.data
drwxr-xr-x 2 bob users 512 Sep 28 14:49 tpsreports
$ ls -la
total 2532
drwxr-xr-x 4 bob sales 512 Sep 28 14:56 .
drwxr-xr-x 14 root root 512 Sep 27 08:43 ..
-rw-r--r-- 1 bob users 28 Sep 28 14:22 .profile
-rw------- 1 bob users 3314 Sep 28 14:56 .bash_history
-rw-r--r-- 1 bob sales 25628 Sep 27 08:54 lecture.mp3
drwxr-xr-x 3 bob users 512 Sep 28 09:20 PerfReviews
-rw-r--r-- 1 bob users 10400 Sep 27 08:52 sales.data
drwxr-xr-x 2 bob users 512 Sep 28 14:49 tpsreports
$ ls -al
total 2532
drwxr-xr-x 4 bob sales 512 Sep 28 14:56 .
drwxr-xr-x 14 root root 512 Sep 27 08:43 ..
-rw-r--r-- 1 bob users 28 Sep 28 14:22 .profile
-rw------- 1 bob users 3314 Sep 28 14:56

.bash_history
-rw-r--r-- 1 bob sales 25628 Sep 27 08:54 lecture.mp3
drwxr-xr-x 3 bob users 512 Sep 28 09:20 PerfReviews
-rw-r--r-- 1 bob users 10400 Sep 27 08:52 sales.data
drwxr-xr-x 2 bob users 512 Sep 28 14:49 tpsreports

Listing Files by Type

When you use the -F option for ls a character is appended to the file name that reveals what type it is.

$ ls
dir1 link program regFile
$ ls -F
dir1/ link@ program* regFile
$ ls -lF
total 8
drwxr-xr-x 2 bob users 117 Sep 28 15:31 dir1/
lrwxrwxrwx 1 bob users 7 Sep 28 15:32 link@ -> regFile
-rwxr-xr-x 1 bob users 10 Sep 28 15:31 program*
-rw-r--r-- 1 bob users 750 Sep 28 15:32 regFile

Symbol	Meaning
/	Directory.

Symbol	Meaning
@	Link. The file that follows the -> symbol is the target of the link.
*	Executable program.

A link is sometimes called a symlink, short for symbolic link. A link points to the location of the actual file or directory. You can operate on the link as if it were the actual file or directory. Symbolic links can be used to create shortcuts to long directory names. Another common use is to have a symlink point to the latest version of installed software as in this example.

bob@linuxsvr:~$ cd /opt/apache
bob@linuxsvr:/opt/apache ~$ ls -F
2.3/ 2.4/ current@
bob@linuxsvr:/opt/apache$ ls -l
drwxr-xr-x 2 root root 4096 Sep 14 12:21 2.3
drwxr-xr-x 2 root root 4096 Nov 27 15:43 2.4
lrwxrwxrwx 1 root root   5 Nov 27 15:43 current -> 2.4

Listing Files by Time and in Reverse Order

If you would like to sort the ls listing by

time, use the -t option.

```
$ ls -t
tpsreports
PerfReviews
lecture.mp3
sales.data
$ ls -lt
total 2532
drwxr-xr-x 2 bob users  512     Sep 28 14:49
tpsreports
drwxr-xr-x 3 bob users  512     Sep 28 09:20
PerfReviews
-rw-r--r-- 1 bob sales 2562856 Sep 27 08:54
lecture.mp3
-rw-r--r-- 1 bob users  10400   Sep 27 08:52
sales.data
```

When you have a directory that contains many files it can be convenient to sort them by time, but in reverse order. This will put the latest modified files at the end of the ls output. The old files will scroll off the top of your display, but the most recent files will be right above your prompt.

```
$ ls -latr
total 2532
drwxr-xr-x 14 root root 512   Sep 27 08:43 ..
-rw-r--r-- 1 bob users 10400  Sep 27 08:52
sales.data
```

```
-rw-r--r-- 1 bob sales 256285 Sep 27 08:54 lecture.mp3
drwxr-xr-x 3 bob users    512 Sep 28 09:20 PerfReviews
-rw-r--r-- 1 bob users     28 Sep 28 14:22 .profile
drwxr-xr-x 2 bob users    512 Sep 28 14:49 tpsreports
drwxr-xr-x 4 bob sales    512 Sep 28 14:56 .
-rw------- 1 bob users   3340 Sep 28 15:04 .bash_history
```

Listing Files Recursively

Using the -R option with ls causes files and directories to be displayed recursively.

```
$ ls -R
.:
PerfReviews lecture.mp3 sales.data tpsreports
./PerfReviews:

Fred John old

./PerfReviews/old:
Jane.doc
$
```

You can also use the tree command for more visually appealing output. If you only want to see the directory structure, use tree -d .

tree - List contents of directories in a tree-like format.

tree -d - List directories only.

tree -C - Colorize output.

```
$ tree
```

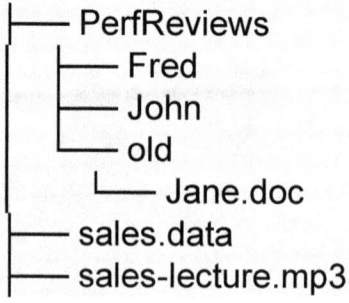

```
.
├── PerfReviews
│   ├── Fred
│   ├── John
│   └── old
│       └── Jane.doc
├── sales.data
├── sales-lecture.mp3
```

└── tpsreports

2 directories, 6 files
$ tree -d
.
└── PerfReviews
    └── old

2 directories
$

List Directories, Not Contents

Normally when you run ls against a directory the contents of that directory are displayed. If you want to ensure you only get the directory name, use the -d option.

$ ls -l PerfReviews
total 3
-rw-r--r-- 1 bob users 36 Sep 27 08:49 Fred
-rw-r--r-- 1 bob users 36 Sep 28 09:21 John
drwxr-xr-x 2 bob users 512 Sep 27 12:40 old
$ ls -ld PerfReviews
drwxr-xr-x 3 bob users 512 Sep 28 09:20 PerfReviews
$ ls -d PerfReviews
PerfReviews

Listing Files with Color

Earlier you used ls -F to help differentiate file types by adding a character to the end of their names in the ls output. You can also use color to distinguish file types by using ls --color.

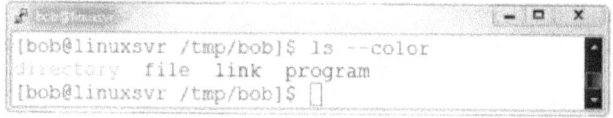

Commonly Used ls Options

Here is a recap of the ls options you have learned.

Option	Description
-a	All files, including hidden files
--color	List files with colorized output
-d	List directory names and not their contents
-l	Long format
-r	Reverse order
-R	List files recursively
-t	Sort by time, most recently modified first

Working with Spaces in Names

If you want to make your life easier when working from the command line, do not use spaces in file and directory names. Hyphens (-) or underscores (_) can be good substitutes for spaces. CamelCase, the practice of capitalizing each word, is another good option. For example, instead of naming your latest literary attempt "the next great american novel.txt" you could use "the-next-great-american-novel.txt", "the_next_great_american_novel.txt" or even "TheNextGreatAmericanNovel.txt."

Sooner or later you will encounter a file or directory that contains a space in the name. There are two ways to deal with this. The first is to use quotation marks. Even though the file name is a file, operate on it using "a file." The second option is to escape the space. Escaping is like using quotes, but for single characters. The escape symbol is \ , also known as a backslash. To escape a space, precede the space with the backslash (\ ) character.

```
$ ls -l
-rw-r--r-- 1 bob users 18 Oct 2 05:03 a file
$ ls -l a file
ls: a: No such file or directory
ls: file: No such file or directory
$ ls -l "a file"
-rw-r--r-- 1 bob users 18 Oct 2 05:03 a file
$ ls -l a\ file
-rw-r--r-- 1 bob users 18 Oct 2 05:03 a file
$ ls -lb a*
-rw-r--r-- 1 bob users 18 Oct 2 05:03 a\ file
$
```

The -b option to ls causes it to print escape codes. Note that quoting and escaping not only applies to spaces, but with other special characters as well including | & ' ; ( ) < > space tab .

Deep Dive

- Escaping Special Characters in Linux and Unix: With 7 Practical Examples - An article that takes a in-depth look at escaping. http://linuxg.net/escaping-special-characters-in-linux-and-unix-with-7-practical-examples/

- man bash - Look at the "QUOTING" section for handling special characters including spaces.

- man ls - To learn about all of the available options to ls refer to the man page.

WHAT'S NEXT

This series continues with Day 2 availabe at:
http://www.linuxtrainingacademy.com/day2

ABOUT THE AUTHOR

Jason Cannon started his career as a Unix and Linux System Engineer in 1999. Since that time he has utilized his Linux skills at companies such as Xerox, UPS, Hewlett-Packard, and Amazon.com. Additionally, he has acted as a technical consultant and independent contractor for small to medium businesses.

Jason has professional experience with CentOS, RedHat Enterprise Linux, SUSE Linux Enterprise Server, and Ubuntu. He has used several Linux distributions on personal projects including Debian, Slackware, CrunchBang, and others. In addition to Linux, Jason has experience supporting proprietary Unix operating systems including AIX, HP-UX, and Solaris.

He enjoys teaching others how to use and exploit the power of the Linux operating system and teaches online video training courses at http://www.LinuxTrainingAcademy.com.

Jason is also the author of *Python Programming for Beginners* and *Command Line Kung Fu: Bash Scripting Tricks, Linux Shell Programming Tips, and Bash One-Liners*

OTHER BOOKS BY THE AUTHOR

For a complete list of Jason's books visit his author page at:
http://www.amazon.com/author/jasoncannon

Command Line Kung Fu: Bash Scripting Tricks, Linux Shell Programming Tips, and Bash One-liners
http://www.linuxtrainingacademy.com/command-line-kung-fu-book

High Availability for the LAMP Stack: Eliminate Single Points of Failure and Increase Uptime for Your Linux, Apache, MySQL, and PHP Based Web Applications
http://www.linuxtrainingacademy.com/ha-lamp-book

Python Programming for Beginners
http://www.linuxtrainingacademy.com/python-programming-for-beginners

ADDITIONAL RESOURCES INCLUDING EXCLUSIVE DISCOUNTS FOR YOU

For even more resources, visit: http://www.linuxtrainingacademy.com/resources

Books

Command Line Kung Fu
http://www.linuxtrainingacademy.com/command-line-kung-fu-book

Do you think you have to lock yourself in a basement reading cryptic man pages for months on end in order to have ninja like command line skills? In reality, if you had someone share their most powerful command line tips, tricks, and patterns you'd save yourself a lot of time and frustration. This book does just that.

High Availability for the LAMP Stack

http://www.linuxtrainingacademy.com/ha-lamp-book

Eliminate Single Points of Failure and Increase Uptime for Your Linux, Apache, MySQL, and PHP Based Web Applications

Python Programming for Beginners
http://www.linuxtrainingacademy.com/python-programming-for-beginners

If you are interested in learning how to program, or Python specifically, this book is for you. In it you will learn how to install Python, which version to choose, how to prepare your computer for a great experience, and all the computer programming basics you'll need to know to start writing fully functional programs.

Scrum Essentials
http://www.linuxtrainingacademy.com/scrum-book

This book will provide every team member, manager, and executive with a common understanding of Scrum, a shared vocabulary they can use in applying it, and practical knowledge for deriving maximum value from it. After reading Scrum Essentials you will know about scrum roles, sprints, scrum artifacts, and much more.

Courses

High Availability for the LAMP Stack
http://www.linuxtrainingacademy.com/ha-lamp-stack

Learn how to setup a highly available LAMP stack (Linux, Apache, MySQL, PHP). You'll learn about load balancing, clustering databases, creating distributed file systems, and more.

Linux for Beginners
http://www.linuxtrainingacademy.com/lfb-udemy

This is the online video training course based on this book. This course includes explanations as well as real-world examples on actual Linux systems.

Learn Linux in 5 Days

http://www.linuxtrainingacademy.com/linux-in-5-days

Take just 45 minutes a day for the next 5 days and I will teach you exactly what you need to know about the Linux operating system. You'll learn the most important concepts and commands, and I'll even guide you step-by-step through several practical and real-world examples.

Linux Alternatives to Windows Applications

http://www.linuxtrainingacademy.com/linux-alternatives

If you ever wanted to try Linux, but were afraid you wouldn't be able to use your favorite software, programs, or applications, take this course.

LPI Level 1 / Exam 101 Training

http://www.linuxtrainingacademy.com/lpi-course-1

This course provides interactive step-by-step videos that will help you prepare for the LPIC-1 101 Exam. This exam is important to help you prepare for the Linux+ and LPIC level 1 certification and this course provides all the materials you need to pass the exam.

LPI Level 1 / Exam 102 Training
http://www.linuxtrainingacademy.com/lpi-course-2

This course provides interactive, step-by-step videos that will help you prepare for the LPIC-1 102 Exam. This exam is important to help you prepare for the Linux+ and LPIC level 1 certification and this course provides all the materials you need to pass the exam.

Python for Beginners
http://www.linuxtrainingacademy.com/python-video-course

This comprehensive course covers the basics of Python as well as the more advanced aspects such as debugging and handling files. Enroll in this course to gain access to all 13 chapters of this Python for Beginners course as well as labs and code files.

Cloud Hosting and VPS (Virtual Private Servers)

Digital Ocean
http://www.linuxtrainingacademy.com/digitalocean

Simple cloud hosting, built for developers. Deploy an SSD cloud server in just 55 seconds. You can have your own server for as little as $5 a month.

Web Hosting with SSH and Shell Access

Bluehost
http://www.linuxtrainingacademy.com/bluehost

99% of my websites are hosted on Bluehost. Why? Because it's incredibly easy to use with 1-click automatic WordPress installation and excellent customer service - via phone and via chat. I HIGHLY RECOMMEND using Bluehost for your first site. Also, you can use the same hosting account for multiple domains if you plan on creating more websites. Visit http://www.linuxtrainingacademy.com/bluehost to get a special discount off the regular price!

HostGator

http://www.linuxtrainingacademy.com/hostgator

If you want an alternative to Bluehost, check out HostGator. It comes with a 99.9% uptime guarantee and includes a free site builder. They provide customer support 24 hours a day, seven days a week and even provide a 45 day money-back gaurantee..

APPENDICES

APPENDIX A:

ABBREVIATIONS AND ACRONYMS

ACL - access control list

APT - advanced packaging tool (apt)

ASCII - American Standard Code for Information Interchange

CentOS - Community ENTerprise Operating System

cd - Change directory

CLI - command line interface

crontab - cron table

dir - directory

distro - Distribution, a collection of user programs, software, and the Linux kernel to create an operating environment.

FOSS - free open source software

FTP - file transfer protocol

GID - group identification

GB - gigabyte

GNU - GNU's Not UNIX. (See GNU.org)

GUI - graphical user interface

HP - Hewlett-Packard

IBM - International Business Machines

KB - kilobyte

I/O - input/output

LFS - Linux from scratch. (See http://www.linuxfromscratch.org/)

LSB - Linux Standard Base

LUG - Linux user group

LVM - logical volume management

MB - megabyte

MBR - master boot record

NFS - network file system

NTP - network time protocol

OS - operating system

PID - process identification number

POSIX - portable operating system interface

pwd - present working directory

RHEL - RedHat Enterprise Linux

RHCE - Red Hat Certified Engineer

RPM - RedHat Package Manager

SAN - storage area network

SELinux - Security Enhanced Linux

SFTP - secure file transfer protocol or SSH file transfer protocol

SGID - set group ID

SLES - SuSE Linux Enterprise Server

SSH - secure shell

STDIN - Standard input

STDOUT - Standard output

STDERR - Standard error

su - superuser

sudo - superuser do

SUID - set user ID

symlink - symbolic link

tar - tape archive

TB - terabyte

TTY - teletype terminal

UID - user identification

VDI - virtual disk image

X - X window system

YUM - Yellowdog Updater, Modified (yum)

APPENDIX B: FAQ

Q: Where can I access all the links in this book?

The links covered in this book along with other supplemental material is available at:

http://www.linuxtrainingacademy.com/lfb

Q: What is Linux?

Linux is an open-source operating system modelled after UNIX.

Q: What is the Linux kernel?

The Linux kernel handles the interactions between the software running on the system and the hardware. To learn more, visit the official Linux kernel website at http://www.kernel.org.

Q: Which Linux distribution should I use?

If your goal is to eventually become a Linux system administrator, focus on CentOS or Ubuntu. CentOS is a Red Hat Enterprise Linux (RHEL) derivative. As a general rule, CentOS and RHEL are often found in corporate environments. Ubuntu is popular with startups and smaller companies that run their operations in the cloud. If you are using Linux for your own personal reasons, choose a distribution that appeals to you. To get some ideas look at DistroWatch.com's top 10 distributions page.

Here are some other common Linux distributions:

- Arch Linux - https://www.archlinux.org/
- Debian - http://www.debian.org/
- Fedora - http://fedoraproject.org/
- LinuxMint - http://www.linuxmint.com/
- Mageia - http://www.mageia.org/
- openSUSE - http://www.opensuse.org/

There are several special purpose Linux distributions that focus on a single area. Examples areas of focus include education, minimalism, multimedia, networking/firewalls, and security. Here is just a sampling of the available specialty distros.

- ArtistX - A DVD which turns a computer into a full multimedia production studio. http://artistx.org/

- Edubuntu - An education oriented operating system. http://www.edubuntu.com/

- live.linuX-gamers.net - A live Linux distribution focused on gaming. http://live.linux-gamers.net/

- Mythbuntu - Mythbuntu is focused upon setting up a standalone MythTV based PVR (personal video recorder) system. http://www.mythbuntu.org/

- Parted Magic - A Hard disk management solution. https://partedmagic.com/

- Scientific Linux - Scientific Linux is put together by Fermilab, CERN, and various other labs and universities around the world. Its primary purpose is to reduce duplicated effort of the labs, and to have a common install base for the various experimenters.
  https://www.scientificlinux.org/

- Ubuntu Studio - Provides the full range of multimedia content creation applications for audio, graphics, video, photography and publishing.
  http://ubuntustudio.org/

- VortexBox - VortexBox is a multifunctional solution to rip, store and stream CDs, digital music and Internet radio.
  http://www.vortexbox.co.uk/

Q: Can I use Microsoft Office in Linux?

Microsoft Office is not available for Linux, however there are alternatives such as Libreoffice, Open Office, and AbiWord.

Q: How do I run XYZ program in Linux?

To find Linux alternatives for software you use on Mac and Windows, visit http://alternativeto.net/.

APPENDIX C: TRADEMARKS

BSD/OS is a trademark of Berkeley Software Design, Inc. in the United States and other countries.

Facebook is a registered trademark of Facebook, Inc..

Firefox is a registered trademark of the Mozilla Foundation.

HP and HEWLETT-PACKARD are registered trademarks that belong to Hewlett-Packard Development Company, L.P.

IBM® is a registered trademark of International Business Machines Corp., registered in many jurisdictions worldwide.

Linux® is the registered trademark of Linus Torvalds in the U.S. and other countries.

Mac and OS X are trademarks of Apple Inc., registered in the U.S. and other countries.

Open Source is a registered certification mark of Open Source Initiative.

Sun and Oracle Solaris are trademarks or registered trademarks of Oracle Corporatoin and/or its affiliates in the United States and other countries.

UNIX is a registered trademark of The Open Group.

Windows is a registered trademark of Microsoft Corporation in the United States and other countries.

All other product names mentioned herein are the trademarks of their respective owners.

CPSIA information can be obtained
at www.ICGtesting.com
Printed in the USA
LVHW020230140423
744036LV00024B/230